Water Detective

CONTENTS

NATIONAL GEOGRAPHIC
School Publishing
Hampton-Brown

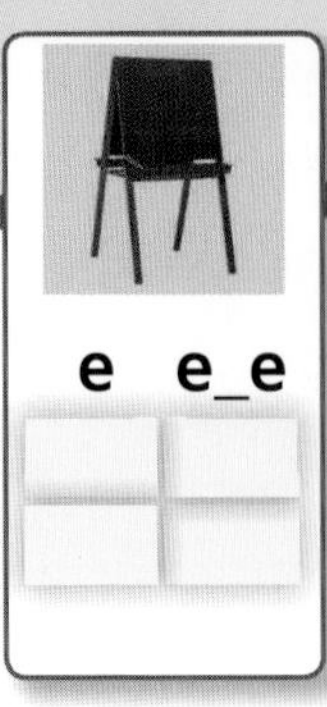

Words with Long e

Look at each picture. Read the words.

Example:

me

Pete

Eve

High Frequency Words
clean
going
let
off
our
stop
take
think

Key Words

Look at the picture. Read the invitation.

Can You Come?

1. We are **going** to have water fun at **our** home.
2. You can **stop** by at ten o'clock.
3. **Take** the bus and get **off** at Briggs St.
4. You will go home **clean**!
5. **Let** me know if you **think** you can come.

How do you think you can have water fun?

GO! Phonics Games

NGReach.com

A Day at Water Camp

by Hannah Cone • illustrated by Rob McClurkan

This will be a fun day for me. Our class is going on a trip to Water Camp.

We get on the bus. I sit next to Pete and we look at comics. Steve and Zeke tell jokes.

Eve sings solo because no one else will sing. Before Eve finishes singing, we are at Water Camp.

At the camp, Mr. Cleve tells us we will do some basic tests or experiments with water.

He fills a big basin with water. Then we predict which objects will float and which objects will sink.

Next, Mr. Cleve fills two tubs with water and puts salt in one tub. He gets two eggs.

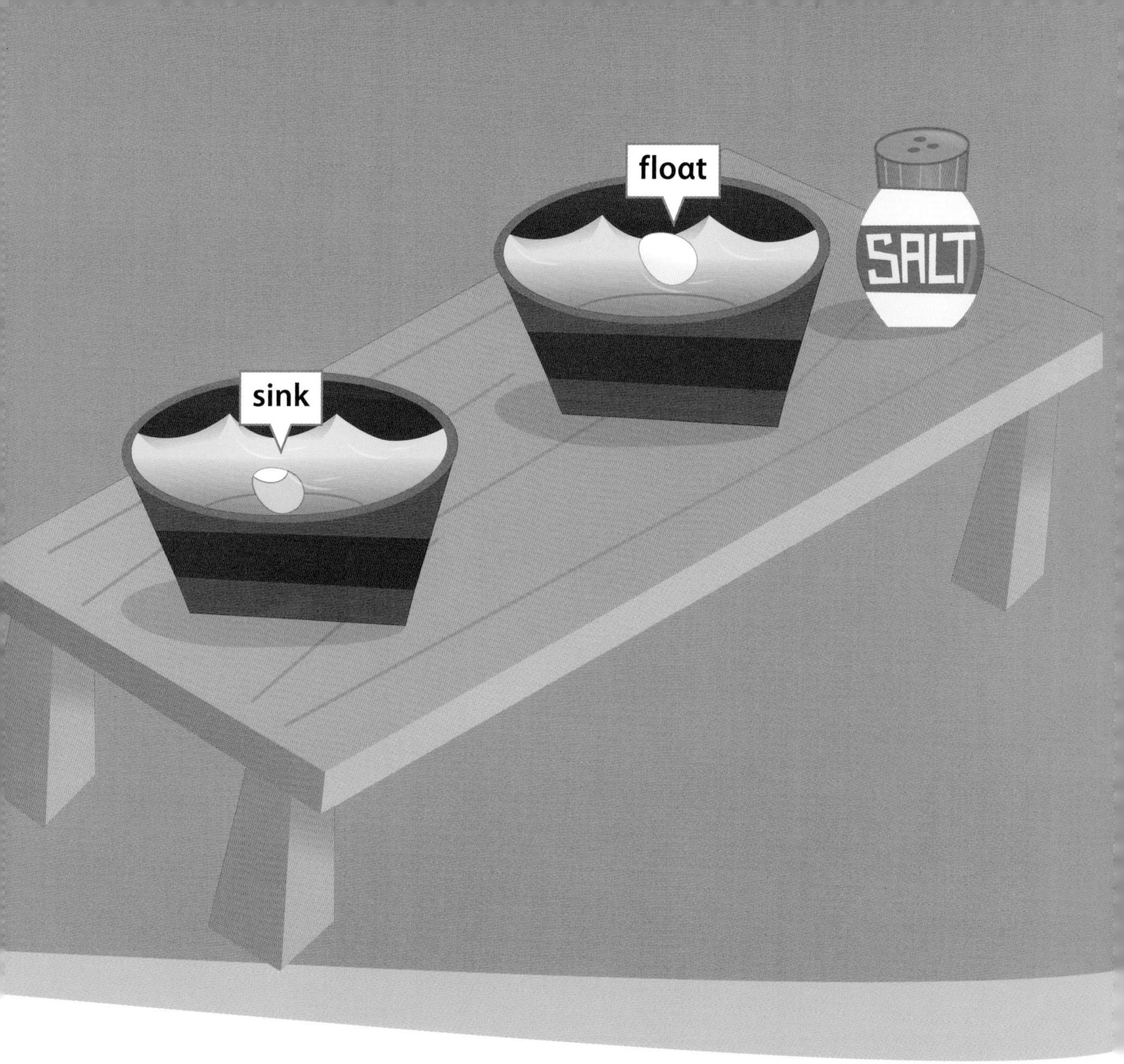

"I will put one egg in each tub. Which egg will sink and which will float?" Mr. Cleve asks.

We find out that the egg in salt water floats.

Then Mr. Cleve fills a tub with water and drops in an orange. It floats.

Mr. Cleve asks, "How can we make this orange sink?"

We find out that if you cut the skin off the orange, it will sink. The skin has air pockets that make it float.

At last, Mr. Cleve takes us to a pond.

He tells us, “Stop and think. Will you float or will you sink? Let’s find out.”

We jump in. We can float *and* sink. It's the best experiment at Water Camp! ❖

Words with Long e̲

Read these words.

he	be	dive	we
fish	she	these	swim

Find the words with long **e**.
Use letters to build them.

h e

Talk Together

Where can we swim?

Choose words from the box to ask your partner about the children and the water.

1.

2.

3.

Endings -s, -ed, -ing

Look at each picture. Read the words.

Example:

claps

smiled

runs

dripping

mopped

riding

High Frequency Words
clean
going
let
off
our
stop
take
think

Key Words

Look at the picture. Read the sentences.

Saving Water

1. I **think** of ways that are **going** to save water in **our** home.
2. I ask Dad to turn **off** the water when he shaves.
3. I ask Mom to **stop** the dripping from the tap.
4. Mom scrubs the dishes, and **lets** me rinse them **clean**.
5. I **take** the hose and water the grass before the sun rises.

How are you going to save water?

Phonics Games
NGReach.com

Ways to Save WATER

by Bo Grayson

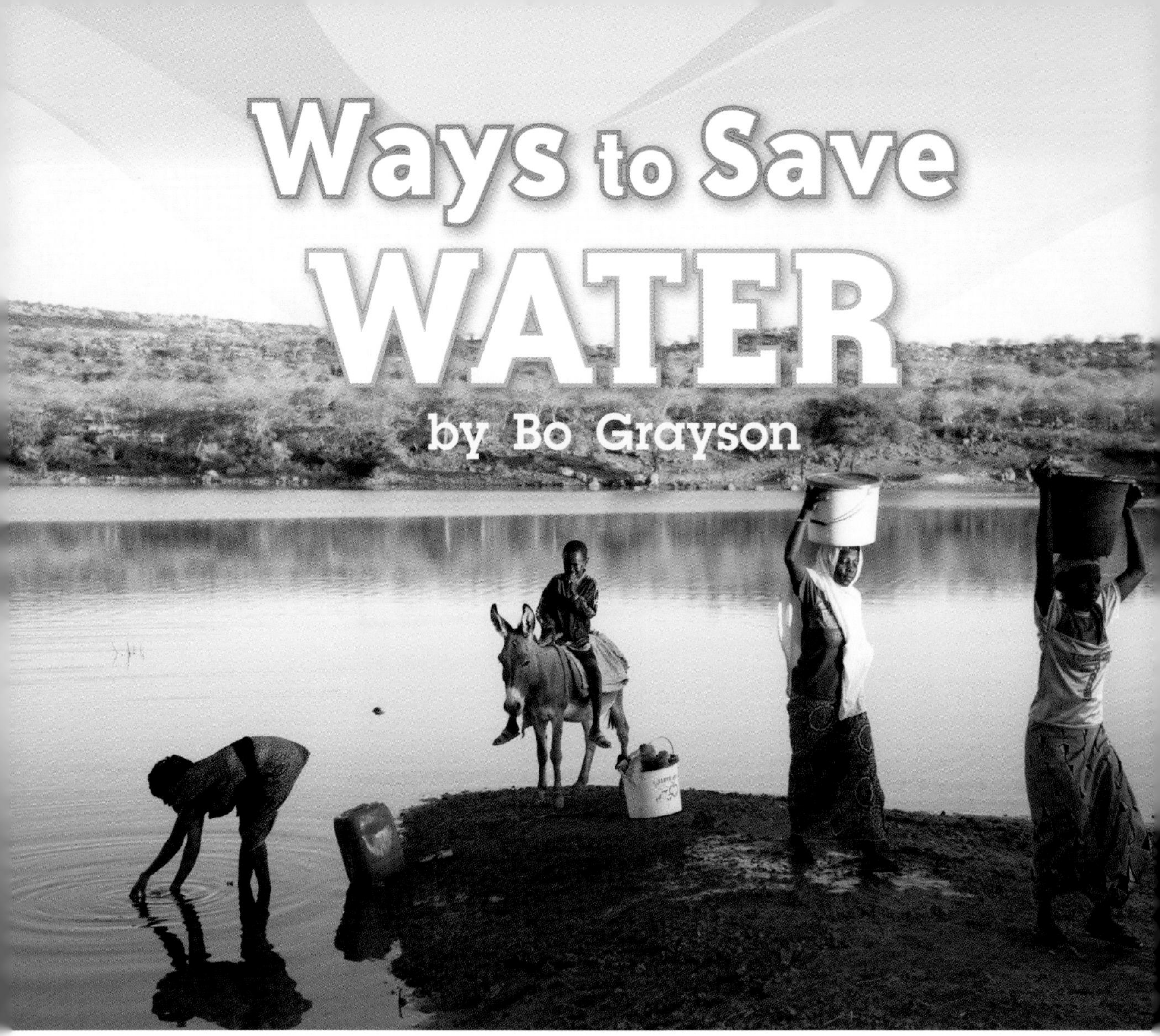

Why Must We Save Water?

There is a limit to how much fresh water is in our world. Each year, more and more people are using water. There is less water for people to drink.

How Can We Save Water?

It takes planning to save water. These are some things you can do inside and outside your home.

Saving Water Inside

Don't have the water running when cleaning dishes. Scrub them and then turn on the water for rinsing.

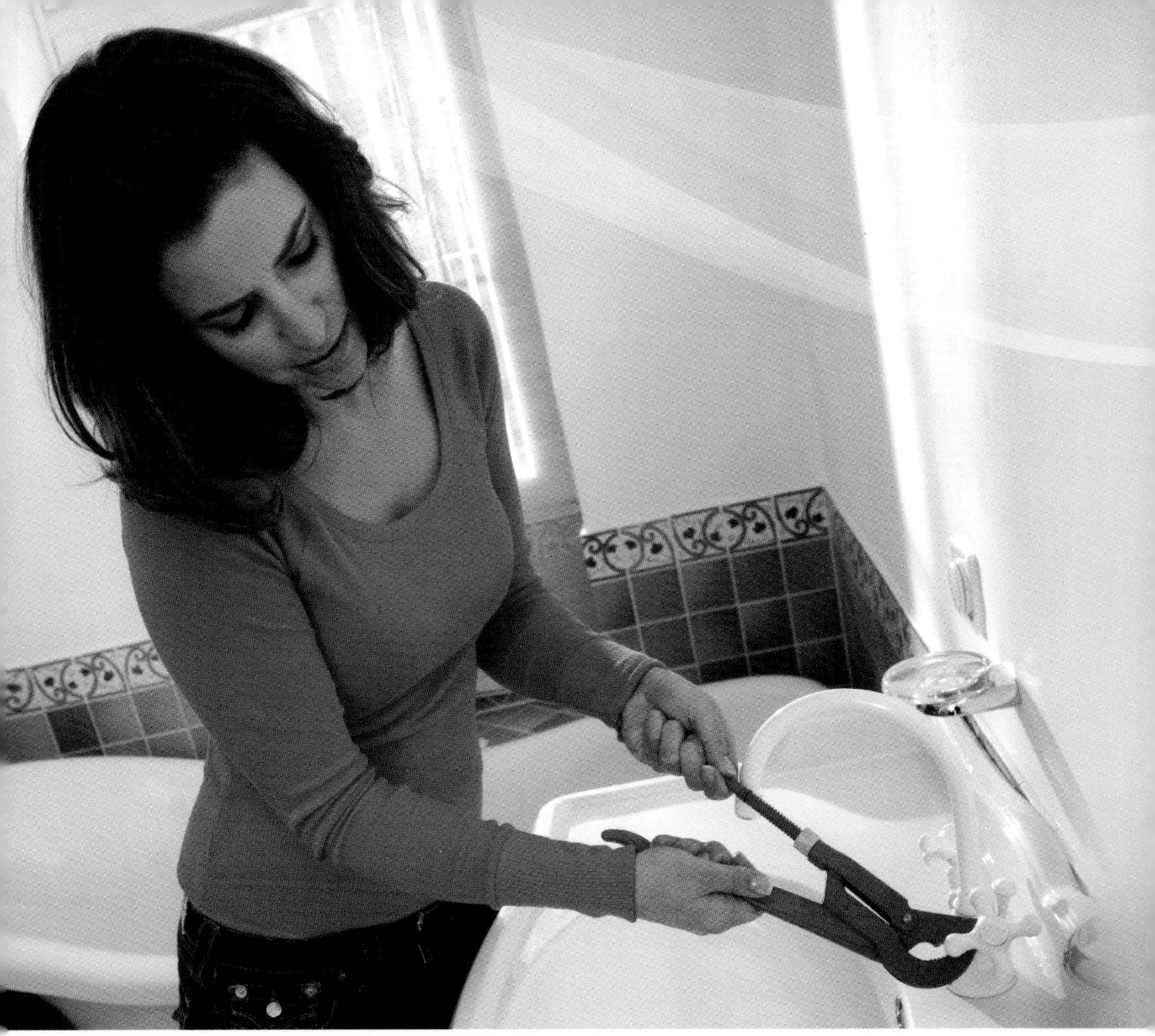

If water is dripping from a tap in the sink, fix the tap.

Water is good for you. Drink a lot of water to stay fit. But do not fill your glass so much you spill and waste the water.

Save drinking water that is left over. Use it to water plants inside.

💧 Turn off the water while brushing.

💧 Take a shower, not a bath. Do not let the tub get plugged up.

Saving Water Outside

Water the plants when it is not too hot.
They will get more water.

If you are going to have fun with a hose, do it on the grass. This way, the grass gets water at the same time.

Add plants that do not need a lot of water. Plant them in spots that are shaded.

Save rain to water plants.

It makes sense to save water. Just think—if each of us helps, then there will be water for all people in the world. ❖

Endings -s, -ed, -ing

Read these words.

base	takes	saving	used
close	habit	shutting	planned

Find the words with the endings **-s**, **-ed**, or **-ing**. Use letters to build them.

t a k e s

Talk Together

Choose words from the box to complete the sentences.

1. I used tap water.
2. I am ________ off the water.
3. This ______ less water than a bath.

1.

2.

3.

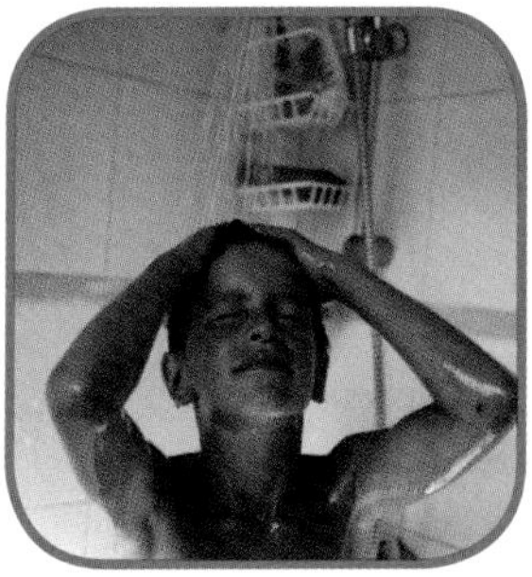

What Are They?

Look at the pictures with a partner. Take turns reading the clues. Then name the objects.

1. Steve and I take the day off. We stop and visit a shop to do some shopping.

2. We each get one of these. Steve gets a red one and I get a yellow one.

3. We clean them and fill them over and over.

4. They are good for going running. They are good for going biking.

5. We even used them at our soccer game. We are glad we stopped and visited that shop!

6. What do you think they can be?

Answer: They are water bottles.

Acknowledgments
Grateful acknowledgment is given to the authors, artists, photographers, museums, publishers, and agents for permission to reprint copyrighted material. Every effort has been made to secure the appropriate permission. If any omissions have been made or if corrections are required, please contact the Publisher.

Photographic Credits
CVR (bg) Studio 1One/Shutterstock. (inset) Radius Images/Alamy Images. **3** Liz Garza Williams/Hampton-Brown/National Geographic School Publishing. **15** (bc) Dennis MacDonald/PhotoEdit. (bl) Jacek Chabraszewski/Shutterstock. (br) BananaStock/Jupiterimages. (t) Liz Garza Williams/Hampton-Brown/National Geographic School Publishing. **16** (bl) Reed Kaestner/Corbis. (br) Blend Images. (cl) BananaStock/Jupiterimages. (cr) Comstock/Jupiterimages. (tl) Jacek Chabraszewski/Shutterstock. (tr) BananaStock/Jupiterimages. **17** (b) Liz Garza Williams/Hampton-Brown/National Geographic School Publishing. (t) DonSmith/Alamy Images. **18** Jim Richardson/National Geographic Image Collection. **19** Nordicphotos/Alamy Images. **20** Izabela Habur/iStockphoto. **21** Denkou Images/Alamy Images. 22 Gerald Bernard/iStockphoto. **23** VikaValter/iStockphoto. **24** (b) Andre Blais/Shutterstock. (t) Inspirestock Inc./Alamy Images. **25** Radius/SuperStock. **26** BananaStock/Jupiterimages. **27** (l) Michael Davis/Garden Picture Library/Photolibrary. (r) Anthony Harris/Shutterstock. **28** (br) Getty Images/Jupiterimages. (l) Bill Aron/PhotoEdit. (tr) PlayPumps International. **29** (bc) Ronnie Kaufman/Larry Hirshowitz/Getty Images. (bl) Nina Shannon/iStockphoto. (br) American Images Inc/Getty Images. (t) Liz Garza Williams/Hampton-Brown/National Geographic School Publishing.

Illustrator Credits
2, **30-31** Scott Burroughs; **4-14** Rob McClurkan

National Geographic School Publishing
Hampton-Brown
www.NGSP.com

Printed in the USA.
RR Donnelley, Menasha, WI

ISBN: 978-0-7362-8066-2

16 17 18 19
10 9 8 7